LIVING WITH CANCER

ABDO
Publishing Company

LIVING
WITH
CANCER

by Genevieve T. Slomski
Content Consultant
Jennifer Reichek, MD, MSW, Attending Oncologist,
Assistant Professor of Pediatrics, Feinberg School of Medicine

LIVING WITH HEALTH CHALLENGES

CREDITS

Published by ABDO Publishing Company, PO Box 398166, Minneapolis, MN 55439. Copyright © 2012 by Abdo Consulting Group, Inc. International copyrights reserved in all countries. No part of this book may be reproduced in any form without written permission from the publisher. The Essential Library™ is a trademark and logo of ABDO Publishing Company.

Printed in the United States of America,
North Mankato, Minnesota
102011
012012

 THIS BOOK CONTAINS AT LEAST 10% RECYCLED MATERIALS.

Editor: Holly Saari
Copy Editor: Karen Latchana Kenney
Series design and cover production: Becky Daum
Interior production: Kazuko Collins

Library of Congress Cataloging-in-Publication Data
Slomski, Genevieve T., 1950-
  Living with cancer / by Genevieve T. Slomski ; content consultant, Jennifer Reichek.
    p. cm.
  Includes bibliographical references.
  ISBN 978-1-61783-124-9
  1. Cancer--Juvenile literature. I. Reichek, Jennifer. II. Title.
  RC264.S56 2012
  616.99'4--dc23
                              2011033151

TABLE OF CONTENTS

EXPERT ADVICE

As a pediatric oncologist, it is my job to take care of adolescents and young adults with cancer. Before attending medical school, I worked for five years as a psychotherapist with adolescents in an inpatient psychiatric unit. This gave me preparation in handling the intense emotional and psychosocial aspects of cancer that many teens experience.

When I started medical school, I knew I wanted to work with kids and teenagers. In my job, I have the privilege of helping young people face tough times in their lives, and I work hard to aid with emotional and medical aspects of the disease—both being important parts for healing.

I know that young people with cancer have many concerns and fears. You might be nervous about your changing appearance and not physically fitting in. Maybe you think you'll be an outcast or made fun of at school. Or you might have long-term concerns about being able to have children in the future. It is important that you discuss your concerns and questions with your medical team and support group. They are there to help you through this time in your life.

The top pieces of advice I have for you are:

Make sure you can talk to your doctor. If you have concerns about your treatment, get a second opinion. Ask questions with and without your parents in the room. No question is weird.

You are not alone. Above all else, remember this. If you do not know where to turn, talk to your doctor, who can help you find emotional or other support. Many teens just like you are living with cancer. You can help each other get through the disease and its treatment.

—*Jennifer Reichek, MD, MSW, Attending Oncologist, Assistant Professor of Pediatrics, Feinberg School of Medicine*

I HAVE WHAT?
CANCER BASICS

Since he was old enough to kick a ball, Charlie was happiest when he was outdoors playing soccer. His dream was to be a professional soccer player when he grew up, and he knew he had to work hard to achieve that goal.

Symptoms of cancer include fatigue and bruising easily.

Usually full of energy both on and off the field, in the past few weeks Charlie didn't feel like himself and had trouble keeping up with his teammates. He couldn't run as fast as he used to. No matter how much he slept the night before, he always felt exhausted. He missed shots that should have been easy. He was so tired that he even fell asleep in class a few times, which didn't make his teachers very happy.

Then mysterious bruises started appearing on his arms and legs, but he didn't remember getting hit by the ball in those places during practice or bumping into anything. Although he feared something was wrong, he was afraid to tell his parents—and even more afraid to tell his coach. He didn't want to stop playing the game he loved, and he didn't want to let his teammates down. Although Charlie's mom noticed the bruises on his arms and legs, she just thought they were the lumps and bumps all kids get. But one day, just a few minutes into practice, Charlie collapsed on the field and was rushed to the emergency room. His illness would no longer remain undiscovered.

CANCER DEFINED: STARTING WITH A SINGLE CELL

There are many different types of cancer. Although the different types of cancers are unique, they all begin the same way—with a single cell. Cancer is a disease that is characterized by an abnormal growth of cells in the body.

The body is made up of millions of cells. Normally, these cells grow, multiply, and die according to a schedule that keeps your body functioning properly. Inside every cell

SYMPTOMS TO WATCH FOR

There are so many different types of cancer that it's nearly impossible to list all the possible symptoms, but some of the main symptoms of the kinds of cancers teens get include the following:

- Changes in speech, vision, or hearing
- Drenching night sweats
- Excessive bleeding or bruising
- Frequent infections
- Loss of appetite
- Lumps or bumps anywhere on the body that don't go away
- Persistent fevers
- Problems with balance
- Severe fatigue
- Severe or frequent headaches
- Shortness of breath
- Unusual pain or swelling in any part of the body
- Vomiting upon waking up

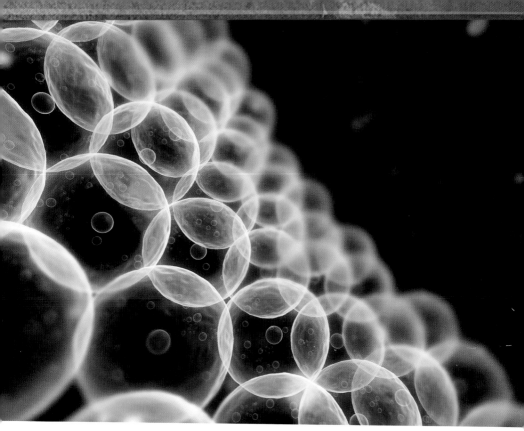

All types of cancer begin with just one abnormal cell.

is deoxyribonucleic acid, or DNA, the genetic material that determines the cell's growth and reproduction. Oftentimes, DNA gets damaged. When this happens in a normal cell, the cell repairs the damage or, if it cannot repair it, the cell dies.

However, sometimes the DNA's damage is not repaired and the cell still lives, becoming an abnormal cell. The abnormal cell can begin multiplying, even though the body doesn't need new cells. The new cells have the damaged DNA and, therefore, continue the process of uncontrollable cell growth. One way to imagine

A BIT MORE ABOUT DNA

DNA is a spiral chain of molecules that carries the genetic information for hereditary traits. You can also think of your DNA as the code or instruction manual each of your cells uses to figure out what function to perform in your body. Your DNA also does something else: it makes copies of itself whenever a new cell is born, so the instruction manual can move into the new cell. DNA can get damaged, however, and if it is not fixed, it can contribute to the growth of cancer cells.

cancer is to see it as cells gone wild—cells that are out of control and can't stop multiplying.

THE ABILITY TO SPREAD

Although cancer starts with one cell, it can metastasize, or spread, to other parts of your body when cells break off from the original location and travel through your bloodstream or lymphatic system. This is how cancer spreads to other body organs. So, a cancer that begins in the lungs can move to the liver and begin growing there as well. Cancer cells can also grow into other tissues, which normal cells cannot do.

MANY DISEASES, MANY SYMPTOMS

Cancer symptoms vary and depend on the type of cancer in the body. In its early stages, many cancers either have no symptoms, or the symptoms are similar to other diseases—such as the flu, for example. In its early stages, a

When damage in a cell's DNA does not repair itself or cause the cell to die, the genetic mutation may begin multiplying uncontrollably.

cancer such as leukemia, cancer of the blood, doesn't form any tumors and works without visible signs on your body. That's why many cancers are not detected early.

Some cancers do have more definitive signs, such as the growth of tumors, which are buildups of cells that form masses of tissue. Tumors can either be benign or malignant.

Many cancers are not detected early because they have no symptoms or ordinary flu-like symptoms.

Not all cancers show up as tumors that are easy to see or feel on the body, though. So if you do notice any symptoms at all, whether they are lumps under the skin or just bruising and drowsiness, don't try to hide them like Charlie. Tell someone right away.

When Charlie's doctors put together all his symptoms—his fatigue, his collapse on the field, and the bruising on his arms and legs, plus the results of the lab tests he received in the emergency room and later—they diagnosed him with acute lymphocytic leukemia (ALL), the most common form of leukemia in children and teens and one that progresses quickly.

YOU'RE MORE THAN YOUR DISEASE

Charlie's oncologist tried to be gentle when he told Charlie's parents and Charlie the news. As soon as he heard the word *cancer*, though, Charlie felt as though someone had just punched him in the gut. He choked back a dozen different emotions. But his oncologist also was quick to tell him that the disease was curable—in fact, most kids with leukemia like his were cured of their disease after treatment.

Just like Charlie, when you hear that you have cancer, you may be shocked and terrified, especially since you're so young. You may have thought that just older people get cancer; you never expected it could happen to you. It can be

TYPES OF CANCER SPECIALISTS

When you have cancer, you'll need a whole team of doctors to treat you. Here are the main types of doctors you may see for treatment:

- **Medical oncologist**—the doctor who oversees your care and who sends you to other specialists.
- **Radiation oncologist**—the doctor who gives you radiation treatment.
- **Surgical oncologist**—the doctor who performs any surgical procedures that you may need, including biopsies that will help diagnose your cancer.

overwhelming, and you have every right to feel all the emotions you're feeling. It's important to remember that you getting cancer had nothing to do with what you did. It is not your fault.

It is tough dealing with everything cancer brings, but with some knowledge, understanding, and support from your friends, family, and medical professionals, you can learn to live with your disease. Remember that you are more than your disease. You are a person who happens to have cancer.

MYTHS ABOUT CANCER

1. *Cancer is sometimes contagious.*
   Cancer is never contagious.
2. *No cancer is ever really cured.*
   Many cancers are effectively treated and cured.
3. *Your hair always falls out when you have cancer.*
   Chemotherapy treatment can cause hair to fall out. However, not all cancers are treated with chemotherapy and not all chemotherapy makes hair fall out.
4. *If you have a family history of cancer, you probably will get it.*
   Most people who get cancer don't have a family history of the disease. Only 5 to 10 percent of all cancers are linked to heredity.[1]

ASK YOURSELF THIS

- *What were your symptoms, and how long did you have them? What prompted you to go to the doctor?*

- *Were you nervous to tell someone about how you were feeling or what you were experiencing? Why?*

- *Before you were diagnosed with cancer, what did you know about the disease?*

- *How did you feel when the doctor first told you that you have cancer? How much time has passed since then? Have your thoughts or feelings changed? How?*

SURVIVING CANCER

Every year in the United States, approximately 12,000 youth between birth and age 19 are diagnosed with cancer—about one in every 300 boys and one in every 333 girls.[2] Although survival rates vary depending on the kind of cancer and how much it has progressed, more and more kids are living longer and getting cured. Scientists and doctors know much more about how to prevent and treat the disease than ever before. Today, the overall five-year relative survival rate of both children and teens is approximately 80 percent.[3]

FINDING OUT FOR SURE: TESTS AND DIAGNOSIS

J ulie's pediatrician diagnosed her with migraines, but the medications her doctor prescribed just didn't seem to work. He tried giving her pills that she had to take every day to try to prevent her headaches. Those didn't work. Then he gave her stronger medications to take when she felt a headache coming on. Those didn't work either.

Julie's headaches were always worse in the morning. When she felt an attack coming on, she would stay in her bedroom, draw the curtains, and lie completely still. She couldn't eat or sleep. She usually felt nauseated and vomited whenever she had a headache, but then she felt a little better. Adding to her stress was her worry over missing so many days of school and feeling that she'd never catch up.

After enduring her intense headaches for nearly a year, Julie began having problems with balance. She stumbled and tripped a lot. Feeling helpless and frustrated, Julie's parents insisted on getting a second opinion and asked Julie's pediatrician to recommend someone. He gave them the name of a neurologist. After reviewing her medical history and giving her a physical exam, the neurologist sent Julie to get several tests to see what was causing her symptoms.

A few weeks later, the doctor told Julie and her parents that he knew what Julie's problem was. She was misdiagnosed. She didn't have migraines; she had a brain tumor. When Julie heard those words, she started crying. She didn't know exactly what it meant, but she thought she would die. She ran out of the doctor's office and made it to the bathroom just in time before throwing up.

YOUR FIRST STOP

When you first start having any symptoms of an illness or a health problem, you'll likely visit your family doctor or pediatrician to find out what's going on. Your doctor will run some tests that may be able to diagnose your cancer. Or he or she may send you to a specialist for more tests. Like Julie's pediatrician, sometimes your family doctor may misdiagnose your illness. Your pediatrician or general practitioner has basic knowledge about a wide range of illnesses and conditions, but they're not cancer experts. If your symptoms continue, talk with your doctor again about seeing someone else so you can find more answers.

TESTS AND MORE TESTS

Although your pediatrician or general practitioner may order some standard laboratory tests or X-rays if cancer is suspected, you will eventually need to see an oncologist. The oncologist will take your complete medical history, give you a physical examination, and order lots of tests.

You will probably have your blood and urine tested to look for cancer cells or to make sure your heart, lung, kidneys, and other vital

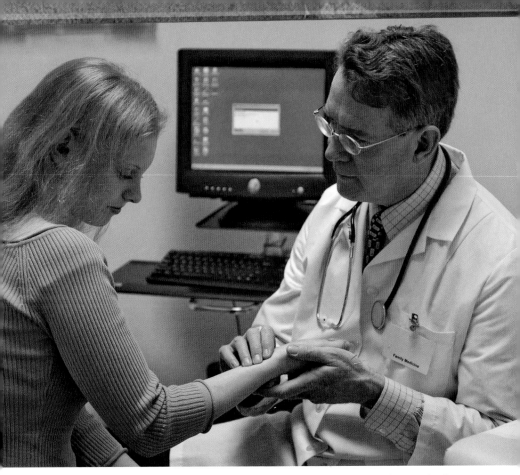

Your doctor will run several tests before referring you to a specialist.

organs are healthy. You may also undergo a few imaging tests, including an ultrasound, X-rays, CT scans, and MRIs. Doctors use these tests to view the bones and organs more closely. Another test you may need is a biopsy, which is when a doctor takes a small tissue sample of the suspect area. For example, to diagnose leukemia, a biopsy is taken from a piece of bone, usually from the hip. Your doctor may use a needle to remove tissue or a

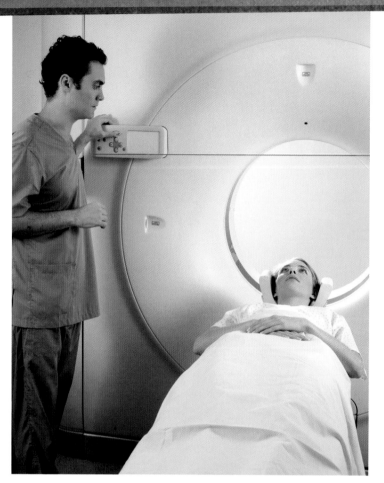

If cancer is suspected, you will get a more comprehensive physical examination and a lot more tests, including a CT scan.

small camera with a tiny surgical tool attached, called a laparoscope, to surgically remove a tiny piece of tissue through a small hole. But sometimes your doctor needs to take a larger tissue sample and will have to perform a more invasive surgical procedure. In some cancers that involve a solid tumor, your doctor may remove your entire tumor during your surgical biopsy. You will probably be under general anesthesia, so you will not feel the biopsy when it happens. However, there is an incision and the biopsy may be pretty invasive, so there is some discomfort or pain after waking up.

After your doctors complete all of their tests, they will review the results to be sure about the kind of cancer you have, where it's located, and the state of your general health. This review of information is important because the results of one test may cause your doctors to go back and reevaluate the results of an earlier test. Your diagnostic team, the team of doctors that may include your general practitioner, oncologist, surgeon, and more medical staff, will put all the pieces of the puzzle together.

HANDLING THE DIAGNOSIS

Once everything is known, your doctor will meet with you and your parents or guardians. For many kids, hearing they have cancer is a severe shock, but

RELAXING DURING AN MRI

During an MRI, you lie very still on a padded table inside a large metal tube that is open at your head and feet. You will be given earplugs or headphones to decrease the loud knocking sound you will hear coming from the machine during the test, which will take up to an hour. Since you will be lying in the small tube for that long, you may get a bit claustrophobic. Try to stay calm by taking slow, deep breaths.

initial reactions can vary. Some kids start crying and others feel nauseous and get sick, like Julie. They may think, *Why me?*, wracking their brains to figure out what they did that caused them to develop cancer. A lot of kids want to know if they're going to die and how long they have to live.

This can be a very scary time for you and your parents. During this meeting with your doctor, you can ask as many questions as you want to find out more about what having cancer means, but you may be too shocked to think of questions to ask. At any time, you can contact your medical team for more information.

After informing you of your cancer, your doctor will also discuss the severity of your cancer by talking about the prognosis of the disease. Hearing your prognosis can be scary. Knowing there is even a small chance that you might not survive or that you might have to have part of a limb amputated (as may be the case

"My whole family was there—my parents, Trey, and my sister, Erin. . . . And the doctors just told us that what I had was Hodgkin's disease. I remember that when they said that, I wasn't sure if it was bad news or not. I hadn't ever heard of Hodgkin's disease. But my parents and my sister started crying. And then the doctors explained that it was a form of cancer. And I didn't cry as much as they did—I just had this one tear. That was it."[1]

—*Kristin, a cancer patient, describing when she was first diagnosed* in a certain type of bone cancer) is terrifying and can feel like too much for you to handle all at once. Your doctor or other hospital staff can recommend therapists and support groups to talk to about this.

The good news is that overall, doctors are happy about the prospects for survival for teen cancer patients. Survival rates are better now than at any time before, as one health worker commented on teen cancer:

QUESTIONS TO ASK YOUR DOCTOR AFTER DIAGNOSIS

- What is the recovery rate for this type of cancer and for me specifically?
- What is the necessary treatment?
- How long will treatment take?
- What are the side effects of treatment?
- How much time in the hospital is necessary?
- Can I still go to school while undergoing treatment?
- What is my prognosis?

Some of these cancers were so serious that the diagnosis was virtually a death sentence ten or fifteen years ago. . . . And others, like osteosarcoma [bone cancer], were a guaranteed amputation. But those things are changing. More than 70 percent of teenagers and other kids with cancer are surviving now, achieving that status of being cured.[2]

A friend may help comfort you when you first learn you have cancer.

While talking with your doctor, you will also learn about the procedures and treatments you will undergo. You may learn that your treatment will take months or possibly years until you fully recover, which can be disheartening and overwhelming to hear. You will probably have tons of thoughts going through your head: What does that mean for school? How will I get to see my friends? Will I have to start living in a hospital? You will deal with these things as they come up, but right now, after the diagnosis, the most important thing is to focus on starting treatment and getting better.

ASK YOURSELF THIS

- *When were you first told that you needed to be tested for cancer? How did you feel? What were your concerns?*

- *What tests did you undergo? How did you feel during each of them?*

- *How would you describe the testing and diagnostic process to a friend who needed to go through the same thing?*

- *How did you react when you first learned you had a cancer diagnosis?*

STAGING YOUR CANCER

Once cancer has been found in your body, doctors will stage your cancer, which means they determine how much cancer you have in your body and if your cancer has spread anywhere. One common way to stage, or rate, the development of cancer is Overall Stage Grouping, which stages cancer ranging from I to IV and recurrent, with the higher numbers being assigned to more severe and widely spread cancer. After the staging process is completed, your doctor can tell whether your disease is still in its original location or whether it has spread to other parts of your body. Your doctor can also give you a more accurate prognosis and determine what treatment is best for you.

DID I DO SOMETHING WRONG? CANCER IN TEENS

Ahmad always brought some music to listen to during his chemotherapy sessions, which took hours. But today, when he sat down at the only empty recliner left in the room, he noticed a really pretty girl with

*For most cancers in young people, the causes are
usually unknown.*

a very bald head in the chair next to him and forgot about his music completely.

"I used to have long, brown hair," she said, looking up at him with huge brown eyes. Now I don't even bother wearing a wig. Bald is beautiful, right?"

"Yes it is," Ahmad said, then asked, "What's your name, and what are you in for?"

"Beth. Non-Hodgkin lymphoma. How about you?" she asked.

"I'm Ahmad, and mine's AML—acute myelogenous leukemia," he replied.

Ahmad had a great conversation with Beth during their long chemo session and got to know all about her disease and how she was coping with it. Although their cancers were both blood-related, Ahmad's and Beth's symptoms were a little different. Beth told Ahmad about the first symptoms she noticed: the lump just under the right side of her jaw, which turned out to be an enlarged lymph node. She had also been tired all the time. She went to her family doctor when the lump didn't go down after a month or so. Her doctor sent her to a specialist, who gave her more tests, and she was diagnosed with cancer soon after.

Ahmad's symptoms also started with fatigue and other flu-like signs. He had a fever, his

Unlike cancer in teens, many cases of cancer in adults have direct causes, such as smoking.

bones ached, and he didn't have an appetite. At first, his mother thought he just had a lingering cold, but when he saw his doctor for his annual physical exam, blood tests showed an abnormally high number of white blood cells. That's when his doctor first suspected leukemia.

CANCER IN YOUNG PEOPLE

In adults, environment, genetics, and lifestyle choices play a role in the development of cancer. For example, people who are near toxins for a long period of time or who smoke and do not exercise are more likely to get certain types of cancer than those who do not do those things. However, this is not the case with cancer in young people. The cancers young people develop are not those that adults are most likely to develop, such as breast, lung, or colon cancer.

The question of what triggers cancer in young people is one that has puzzled researchers for a long time. For most cancers in young people, the causes are not always known. Because causes are unknown, little can be done to eliminate risk factors—as these are unknown as well—or prevent cancer from developing. What *is* known are the most common cancers in teens: leukemias, lymphomas, brain tumors, and sarcomas.

LEUKEMIAS

Leukemias are a group of blood cancers that begin with white blood cells. Leukemia happens when white blood cells grow uncontrollably in bone marrow, where all blood cells are made. The white blood cells can multiply so much that they crowd out red blood cells and platelets. The two kinds of leukemias that affect teens most are acute lymphocytic leukemia (ALL) and acute myelogenous leukemia (AML), with ALL being the more common of the two. Both forms of leukemia tend to produce similar symptoms, which include anemia and fatigue due to not having enough healthy red blood cells, infections from a compromised immune system that can't function properly due to not having enough healthy white blood cells, and poor blood clotting due to not having enough platelets. Chemotherapy is the main form of treatment for leukemias.

LYMPHOMAS

Lymphomas are cancers of the lymphatic system, a bodily system that keeps fluids in balance and fights foreign invaders to protect you from infection. It includes the lymph nodes, spleen, thymus, adenoids, tonsils, and bone marrow. The main lymphomas that teens get are Hodgkin lymphomas (HL) or non-Hodgkin lymphomas (NHL). NHL is the more common of the two types. Teens and young adults get lymphomas more often than adults. HL rarely occurs outside the lymph nodes. In NHL, the affected lymph nodes are more widely scattered throughout the body,

YOUR SPLEEN

The spleen is a soft, fist-sized organ located in the abdominal area on the left side of your body just under your rib cage. The organ helps regulate the amount of blood in your body. It also stores platelets, which help your blood clot, and plays an important role in helping your immune system work properly. The spleen is part of the lymphatic system and can become enlarged when a person has lymphoma.

and the cancer is often found outside the lymph nodes.

Although you may not experience any symptoms of HL at all in its early stages, you may experience symptoms that resemble the flu, such as fever, cough, night sweats, weight loss, or swollen lymph nodes—usually in the abdomen, groin, neck, or armpit. NHL has similar symptoms, with the addition of abdominal pain, nausea, vomiting, and seizures. Lymphomas are often treated with chemotherapy and radiation therapy.

BRAIN TUMORS

Brain cancers are more common in young children but can also occur in teens. Brain

LEUKEMIA AND LYMPHOMA FACTS

1. The incidence (the number of new cancers diagnosed in any year) of ALL and AML is higher in children under 14 than in those over 15.[1]
2. From 2003 to 2007, the incidence of ALL in teens who were 15 to 19 was more than double the incidence of AML.[2]
3. Most of those under 19 with ALL will become five-year survivors of the disease.[3]
4. Older children and teens are more often diagnosed with HL than younger children.[4]
5. The five-year relative survival rate for those under 19 years of age with NHL is 84.1 percent.[5]
6. In those under 20, the five-year relative survival rate with HL is 96.1 percent.[6]

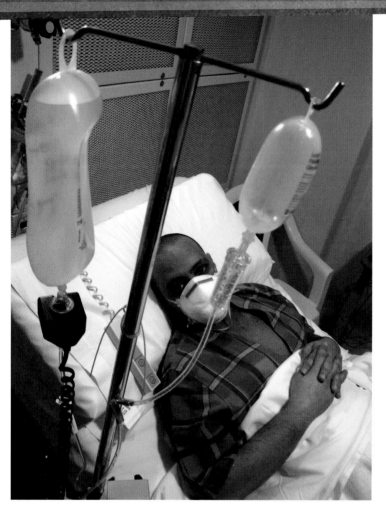

A patient with HL rests in his room. Teens and young adults get lymphomas more often than adults.

tumors can originate in astrocytes or in the lining of the brain's ventricles. Symptoms of a brain tumor include headaches, nausea, vision or speech problems, and depression. Surgery is the main treatment for brain tumors. Chemotherapy and radiation therapy are also used in the instance of a tumor, regardless of whether it is completely removed during surgery.

SARCOMAS

Although rare, teens may also get sarcomas, which are cancers that grow in connective tissue—muscle, cartilage, tendons, or bone. Most often, teens get osteosarcomas, Ewing's sarcomas, and rhabdomyosarcomas.

Osteosarcomas occur in bone, most often in the area just above the knee. The area affected usually feels tender and swollen. Researchers believe the reason why this cancer affects so many adolescents is because they experience periods of rapid bone growth—growth spurts—during adolescent years. This is the time when bones are most vulnerable to damage. Treating osteosarcomas usually involves chemotherapy and surgery, which involves removing the part of the bone that is cancerous. Often a surgeon can replace the bone with a bone graft or special

SARCOMA FACTS

Osteosarcoma. It is estimated that 75 percent of people with osteosarcomas are under 25 years of age and that the disease strikes boys more often than girls.[7] In teens, the disease strikes most often between the ages of 14 and 16.[8]

Ewing's Sarcomas. The average age for developing this cancer is 14 to 15.[9] It is ten times more common in Caucasians than in other ethnicities.[10]

Rhabdomyosarcomas. Boys tend to get this disease slightly more often than girls.[11] When this cancer is diagnosed at an early stage, the overall five-year survival rate is 70 percent.[12]

A patient with Ewing's sarcoma shows where he gets chemotherapy on his body.

metal rod. This prevents amputation. However, sometimes amputation of part or all of a limb may be necessary.

Ewing's sarcomas occur in bone and soft tissue and most often appear in your pelvis, ribs, or upper arms. Scientists are not sure what cells these sarcomas originate in. The most common symptoms are pain and swelling. Ewing's sarcomas are treated with chemotherapy, radiation therapy, and surgery.

Rhabdomyosarcomas start in the skeletal muscles—those responsible for voluntary movement in your body, such as when you move your arms and legs—and can occur anywhere in your body but most often occur in the muscles of your head, neck, bladder, arms, legs, or torso. Rhabdomyosarcomas are treated with chemotherapy and radiation therapy or surgery.

Although the causes of cancers in teens and young people are not fully known, treatments are better than ever and are improving all the time.

ASK YOURSELF THIS

- *What type of cancer do you have? How much do you know about it?*

- *Are you interested in learning more about your cancer? Where can you go to find more information?*

- *Have you talked with any other teens your age who have your type of cancer? What have you learned from them?*

- *Have you talked with your doctor about the prognosis for your type of cancer? What has he or she said?*

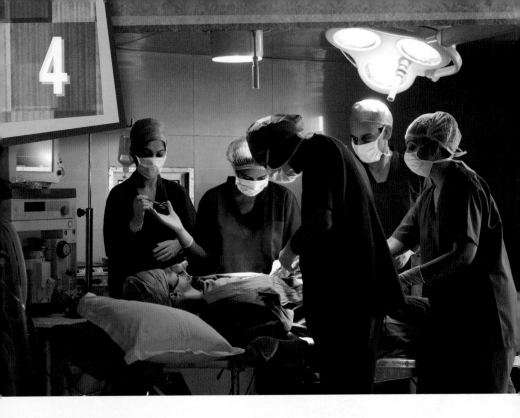

GETTING RID OF YOUR CANCER: TREATMENT

As the nurse wheeled him into the operating room, Brian's thoughts turned to the past year and how much his life had changed since he was first diagnosed with cancer. He couldn't believe that not so long ago his biggest problem was trying to keep his

Many treatment plans will involve an individualized combination of treatments such as chemotherapy, radiation therapy, and surgery.

grades up between lacrosse practices. As he lay on the gurney, about to face surgery, he was scared, and he didn't know what the future had in store for him.

Brian had osteosarcoma in his right knee joint and was about to have knee-replacement surgery. Like most teens with osteosarcoma, Brian had to go through chemotherapy treatments for a few months so the doctors could try shrinking his tumor before surgery. The chemo worked. His tumor got a lot smaller, and when he got his strength back, his doctors scheduled him for surgery.

Brian wasn't so much afraid of the surgery; he was more afraid that it would take him a long time to walk again and get back to "normal." His doctors told him he would need a lot of physical therapy to get his knee working again after surgery. As the doctors placed the mask over his face in the operating room, he heard his mother's voice in his head say, "One step at a time. Just focus on right now. That's all you need to do."

TYPES OF TREATMENT

The kind of cancer treatment Brian received depended on a lot of things: where his cancer

Each cycle of chemotherapy usually lasts between three and four weeks.

was located, the size of his tumor, the type of cancer he had, the stage and grade of his cancer, and his general health. Like Brian, most people with cancer need to have more than one type of treatment. Although there are many possible ways to treat your cancer, the most common treatments are chemotherapy, radiation therapy, and surgery. Your oncologist will design a cancer treatment plan especially for you.

CHEMOTHERAPY

In chemotherapy treatment, often called chemo, doctors give you drugs that help destroy your cancer cells. The drugs can be given in pill or liquid form or by injection into a vein. This kind of treatment is called systemic because the drugs go into your bloodstream and target cells in your whole body. Specifically, the drugs target cells that grow and divide rapidly, such as your cancer cells.

A cycle of chemotherapy usually lasts approximately 21 to 28 days. Usually you'll go to the hospital for a few hours several days a week for a cycle of treatment. Then you'll take a break for a few weeks to give your body a rest. You'll go back for a few weeks for another cycle of treatment. Some teens are admitted to the hospital to receive their chemo, though, especially those with solid tumors and AML. Your doctor will decide on your treatment schedule, depending on how your body responds to the drugs. If you have a solid tumor, chemo may shrink the tumor enough to avoid more extensive surgery.

In Brian's case, shrinking the tumor meant the difference between getting a knee replacement and having his leg amputated because of how the cancer spread. In addition to getting chemo before your surgery, you'll probably receive chemotherapy after surgery to make sure that any remaining cancer cells are destroyed. This kind of chemotherapy is called adjuvant chemotherapy.

Although chemotherapy can make your tumor smaller, it can also have unpleasant side effects, because it not only kills rapidly growing and dividing cancer cells but also kills some other rapidly dividing healthy cells as well. The reason chemotherapy can make your hair fall out is because hair cells divide rapidly, so the chemo sometimes destroys those cells. But your hair will grow back. Other side effects you may experience from your chemo include fatigue, infections, bleeding, mouth sores, constipation

CLINICAL TRIALS

Researchers are always studying new ways of preventing and treating diseases. Although many kinds of clinical trials exist, in a cancer treatment trial, researchers evaluate the safety and efficacy of new, experimental drugs or treatments on people with different kinds of cancer. Your oncologist will be able to tell you about clinical trials involving your type of cancer.

To qualify for a clinical trial, you'll have to meet certain study requirements relating to, for example, your physical condition, cancer stage, or prior treatment history. If you do decide to take part, your doctor or a research nurse must discuss the treatment with you so that you understand the trial and the known risks involved. You'll have to sign a consent form verifying that you understand these risks before you can enroll. Make sure that you ask questions and discuss the idea with your family before you make your decision. If you do decide to take part, it is important to know that you can withdraw from the trial at any time for any reason.

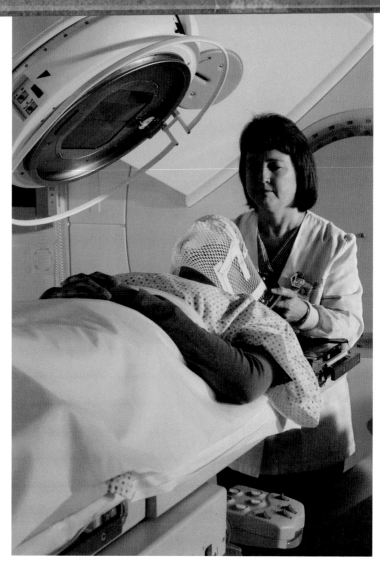

Different cancers need different doses of radiation.

or diarrhea, vomiting, and nausea. Not everyone experiences these symptoms, but if you do, most of the time these symptoms go away after your chemo is over. Your doctor can prescribe medications that lessen the side effects of chemotherapy.

RADIATION THERAPY

Radiation therapy is another form of treatment you may undergo. It treats cancer by using a machine that produces high-energy rays—either X-rays or electrons—targeted at the area of your tumor and sometimes at nearby areas to destroy cancer cells and shrink your tumor. The radiation works by destroying the DNA in your cells so the cells can't multiply and instead die. Like chemotherapy, radiation can destroy healthy cells along with cancerous cells, so your radiation oncologist has to weigh the risks versus the benefits when deciding on this treatment. And like chemotherapy, your oncologist may give you radiation treatment before, during, or after surgery to prevent your cancer from coming back.

Osteosarcomas such as Brian's aren't very sensitive to radiation treatment, so his doctors didn't use it. But you may have a type of cancer that responds to radiation, such as a lymphoma. Your doctor may give you this treatment either by itself or in combination with other treatments. Different cancers need different dosages of radiation.

Before you start your therapy, your radiation oncologist will give you a series of imaging scans that may include an ultrasound, CT, or MRI to pinpoint the exact location of your cancer. You need to lie perfectly still while

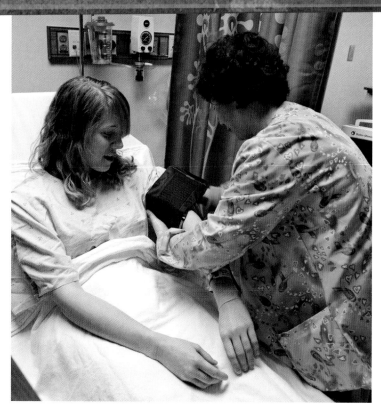

Some teens are admitted to the hospital for treatment, and others commute from home.

you're undergoing radiation treatment so that the radiation targets the exact spot every time you get treatment. So, depending on where your cancer is located, you may have a mold made to keep, for example, your arm, leg, or head in place. You may also get a temporary tattoo pinpointing the spot. The staff involved use computers to plan out all the details of your treatment in advance.

Radiation therapy can cause some of the same side effects as chemo, such as nausea and fatigue, but you may experience other side effects, depending on what part of your body is targeted. These side effects can range from mild to severe, depending on how strong a dosage you need and how long you're treated. Side effects include skin burns, swelling, pain, and numbness where radiation is targeted.

Radiation therapy can also increase your long-term risk of developing certain cancers—especially if you receive this therapy as a child or an adolescent—and heart disease. Radiation can also interfere with bone growth. Your radiation oncologist will give you all the information you need about how radiation works and what kinds of side effects you can expect.

SURGERY

Surgery is often an integral part of therapy for most solid tumors. Doctors perform surgery to remove or reduce your tumor, as in the case of Brian's cancer. But everyone's cancer is different. If, for a variety of reasons, your oncologist doesn't think surgery is possible because of possible damage to a vital organ or because your cancer has spread, he or she may take out as much of the tumor as possible—called debulking—or use chemotherapy, radiation, or both instead.

Over the years, major improvements in cancer surgery have been made. In the past, treatment for an osteosarcoma like Brian's would have likely included the amputation of his whole leg if cancer was found in his knee. These days, it's often possible to have more minimal surgery, like Brian's joint replacement, if your cancer is in a bone or near a joint. If an osteosarcoma is located in the bone above or below the knee, instead of amputation, a surgeon might remove the cancerous part of the bone and some of the healthy tissue around it. Then the surgeon might replace the bone with a specially designed metal replacement called a prosthesis or a bone graft. Sometimes, however, if you have an osteosarcoma, you may need to have your leg amputated if the cancer

WHEN YOU'RE NOT SO HUNGRY

Eating nutritiously is one thing when you're hungry. But if you're having chemo—which sometimes makes food taste metallic—or radiation therapy, you may not feel like eating much of anything. Appetite loss occurs in approximately 15 to 20 percent of all patients when they're diagnosed with cancer and can increase as a result of treatments.[1] Even though you're not hungry, it's important to get some nutrition to keep up your strength during treatment. Your body can't heal if it has no calories to fuel it. Here are some things you can do to get around your lack of appetite:

- Drink instant breakfasts, which contain vitamins, minerals, protein, and antioxidants.
- Eat smaller meals throughout the day rather than one or two big meals.
- Have nutritious foods in liquid form, such as juices, yogurt, or fruit smoothies.
- Sip some beef, chicken, or vegetable broth.
- Try some gelatin; it's easy on your stomach.

When getting treatment, nutritious foods may be easier to consume in liquid form.

has spread from the bone to nearby nerves and blood vessels.

The type of surgery you'll have depends on many factors. Your doctor will discuss all the options with you before you and your parents make a treatment decision. This can be a lot to process and might be the first time you've been faced with decisions of this size. It's okay to feel overwhelmed by all the decisions, but turning to family and experts can help, as can researching the treatment options and making informed choices.

CANCER AND MALNUTRITION

According to the National Cancer Institute, approximately 80 percent of all people with cancer will get some form of malnutrition during the course of their disease.[2] So, it's important for you to maintain a healthy weight and to get enough calories and nutrients into your diet during your cancer treatment.

STAYING HEALTHY DURING TREATMENT

While there are many aspects about your cancer that you cannot control, you can work to keep yourself healthy during your treatment. If you're a typical teen like Brian, you probably eat your share of junk food; however, maintaining a nutritious diet is important in helping your body recover. Skip the chips and eat vegetables and dip instead. Making simple food substitutions is a good step toward eating more nutritiously.

In addition to paying attention to what you eat and avoiding smoking, drinking, and recreational drugs, which you know are bad for your body, physical activity can keep you healthy during your recovery. Exercise has been shown to decrease inflammation and improve the function of the immune system. It's also important to keep your energy up during your cancer treatment, even if it's just walking for 20 minutes a day. Always ask your doctor if you can exercise and how much you should be exercising.

TREATMENT AND FOLLOW-UPS

The total amount of time you will undergo treatment varies on several factors, including your type of cancer, when you were diagnosed, and if cancer recurs once a treatment cycle is complete. Treatment can be as short as just one surgery to as long as three years for ALL in boys, and anywhere in between.

Follow-ups for young people are usually more extensive than follow-ups with adults. After you complete your treatment, you will have

BENEFITS OF YOGA

Doing yoga is a great form of exercise during your cancer treatment. You'll gain strength and flexibility. Plus, you'll get the additional benefit of stress relief and a way to connect your mind, body, and spirit. Many different schools of yoga exist, but they include the practice of deep abdominal breathing; slow, gentle movements or postures; and, sometimes, guided meditation and visualization. Most communities around the country have yoga classes, or you can get a yoga DVD and practice at home.

regular checkups and imaging studies, such as X-rays, for a few years to check on your progress and to make sure that your cancer doesn't come back. This is pretty typical of all cancer patients. However, for children and teens, five years after their diagnosis they are sent to a survivor clinic. This is where they receive outpatient checkups by an oncologist once a year, checking for both side effects from treatment and relapse of the disease. If you have any problems or notice any new symptoms between visits, let your doctor know as soon as possible.

ASK YOURSELF THIS

- *What type of treatment have you had or will you have for your cancer? What else do you know about this type of treatment?*

- *How did you feel before you underwent treatment? If you haven't undergone it yet, what are you feeling leading up to your treatment?*

- *What steps have you taken or are you taking to remain healthy during treatment?*

- *Did your doctor recommend an exercise regimen for you? If so, what is it? How do you feel during and after it?*

5

I DON'T FEEL SO WELL: THE EFFECTS OF TREATMENT

Mia's clothes were strewn about her room. Her closet was basically empty, with its entire contents laid this way and that on her floor and bed.

Weight loss and weight gain during treatment are very common occurrences, so try to be patient when looking for clothes that fit.

"Ugh!" Mia screamed, as she tried to pull on a pair of jeans. She had just gotten them last fall and already they were too small for her.

Since starting chemotherapy five months ago, Mia had gained more than 20 pounds (9 kg). Her clothes didn't fit her anymore and she felt chubby and bloated all the time, not to mention she had joint pain and muscle cramps. But it was really the weight gain that sent her over the edge.

Mia was trying to get ready for her cousin Lisa's birthday. She was just one year younger than Mia, and the two shared a lot of the same friends. Mia hadn't been in school since she started her chemotherapy and was excited to see everyone. But after glimpsing herself in the mirror in a plethora of outfits that were too tight, she was feeling really insecure.

"Mom," she called down the hall. "Nothing will fit me. There's no way I can go. I look like a sausage in a casing. Everyone is going to stare in disgust."

Mia's mom came into her room. "Honey, we talked about this. You have gained a bit of weight, but that is from the chemo drugs you're on right now. If you want, I can help you explain that to your friends."

"No, mom, that would be weird. I just wish I could be normal for this one day. What if no one recognizes me?" Mia asked.

"Everyone will recognize you. You are still the beautiful Mia you've always been," her mom said. "Why don't you wear this dress?" she asked as she picked up a floral printed pile from the bed. "It's looser fitting, so you'll feel more comfortable."

"Fine," Mia said. "But I don't know how long I'll be able to stay, Mom."

"We can leave whenever you want," Mia's mom said.

YOUR PHYSICAL CHALLENGES

Although the treatments you receive for cancer, such as chemo, radiation, or surgery, are helping you get rid of the disease, the medications and procedures involved can be hard on your body. Learn as much as you can about them and ask your doctor if you have any questions. It can be a lot to handle, so don't be afraid to say when you're in pain or not feeling well. Listen to your body as much as possible, and follow the appropriate steps to ease your discomfort.

*Loss of appetite during chemo
can lead to weight loss.*

WEIGHT FLUCTUATIONS

Depending on your type of cancer and
treatment, you may gain or lose weight during
your treatment and healing process. As in Mia's
case, some drugs can make you gain weight.
Mia was undergoing chemotherapy and was
also receiving steroids. Steroids can help ease
some of your cancer symptoms and enhance
your chemo, but they do have some unwanted
side effects, such as weight gain.

Weight loss is also very common, particularly in people with solid tumors. People generally eat less when undergoing chemotherapy. The treatment can bring nausea and vomiting, which can result in weight loss.

Weight fluctuations can be a lot to handle. As if dealing with the inside of your body not cooperating wasn't enough, now your clothes aren't fitting like they used to. It can seem like the last straw. You might be embarrassed or ashamed of your weight now, but although it's hard to do, try not to be. Explain to your friends why you have gained or lost weight, especially if they are worried. When you're feeling insecure, try to remember that this weight gain is an effect of you getting better. If you're still feeling bad, try talking to a peer who is experiencing the same thing as you.

MONITORING SALT INTAKE

Although there isn't too much you can do to minimize weight gain, you can pay attention to your diet and monitor your salt intake to minimize uncomfortable bloating. Salt will make you retain water and can raise your blood pressure.

NAUSEA AND VOMITING

Symptoms of nausea and vomiting are quite common during chemo or radiation treatment, especially when treating the small intestine or brain. It's usually

Nausea is a common side effect of chemotherapy.

worse a few hours after treatment and tends to get better throughout the course of your treatment. It's important to remember to take in fluids to prevent dehydration. In addition to taking anti-nausea medications your doctor may prescribe, here are a few things you can do to calm your stomach:

- Avoid greasy, heavy, or spicy food.

- Cut a lemon and take a whiff—citrus scents can have a positive effect on your nausea.

- Suck on a peppermint hard candy; peppermint is known to have a calming effect on the digestive tract.

BLEEDING AND BRUISING

If you have a blood cancer such as leukemia or lymphoma or if you're being treated with chemo or radiation for any type of cancer, you may experience more bleeding or bruising than normal. Your bleeding may come from your nose, gums, or rectum, the last six to eight inches (15 to 20 cm) of your large intestine. These symptoms are caused by a low count of platelets, cells that help your blood clot.

In addition to any instructions you get from your doctor on curbing the bleeding, you should avoid aspirin or over-the-counter non-steroidal anti-inflammatory drugs (NSAIDs) such as ibuprofen (Motrin and Advil) or naproxen (Aleve), as these drugs can cause more bleeding. Also avoid contact sports, strenuous exercise, and brushing or flossing your teeth too vigorously.

AROMATHERAPY TO EASE NAUSEA

Aromatherapy is the use of scents or essential oils—concentrated oils from plants—to promote health and well-being. To ease nausea, place a drop or two of peppermint, lavender, or lemon oil on a tissue, your pillow, or in a diffuser. You can find these oils at most health food stores. The oils are powerful and can irritate the skin, so don't use the oils directly on your skin.

When you feel nauseated, certain scents can work against you. Breathing harsh chemicals or the smells of certain foods cooking, such as garlic, can make you feel sicker, so steer clear of strong odors.

Many kids experience extreme exhaustion during treatment.

FATIGUE

Often, you will feel very tired after chemo or radiation treatment. This fatigue is often caused by anemia, which is a decrease in the amount of red blood cells in your body. The fewer red blood cells you have, the less oxygen can get to your tissues and organs. In addition to fatigue, you may be pale and have headaches, dizziness, weakness, or shortness of breath.

Your doctor may prescribe medications to increase your red blood cell count or order a blood transfusion, but these are some things you can do when you feel this way:

- Don't overtire yourself with your daily activities.

- Eat a healthy diet with protein, fresh fruits, and vegetables.

- Keep hydrated by drinking water, tea, and juices; avoid caffeine and alcohol.
- With your doctor's approval, take a multivitamin with iron.

INFECTIONS

If you're having chemo or radiation treatments, you have a high risk of getting infections because your immune system is weakened. If you have a temperature of 101 degrees Fahrenheit (38.3°C), or if you have symptoms such as a rash, a sore throat, chills, or diarrhea lasting more than 24 hours, the situation can be serious, so call your doctor or clinic immediately. Because your white blood cells are too weak to fight your infection, you may need antibiotics or to be admitted to the hospital for monitoring

TO PREVENT INFECTIONS

To protect yourself from infections, you can take the following precautions:

- Avoid having fresh flowers in your room; they can carry mold or bacteria.
- Avoid large groups of people or people with infections such as colds, if possible, or wear a mask when they're around.
- Talk to your doctor before going to the dentist. If your white blood cell count is too low, you may risk infection.
- Try to prevent cuts and scrapes, which can be breeding grounds for infections.
- Wash your hands with soap and warm water regularly.

You might also experience pain during treatment. Talk to you doctor about ways to lessen the pain.

until your temperature lowers to a normal 98.6 degrees Fahrenheit (35.6°C).

PAIN

Cancer itself can cause some pain. If you have radiation therapy or surgery for your cancer, you will experience a certain amount of pain afterward as well. When your anesthesia wears off after surgery, your doctor will give you medications to help you manage your pain.

IS REIKI FOR YOU?

Reiki is a Japanese form of energy medicine used to promote stress relief and healing. A Reiki master usually lays his or her hands on or just above your body and rebalances your chi, which is your life-force energy. You can use Reiki along with other medical or healing techniques to help you relieve your symptoms or to promote healing.

When you leave the hospital, you will be given pain pills or your doctor may just tell you to take NSAIDs if you don't have a bleeding disorder.

SENSITIVITY

If you need radiation treatments, you may experience some side effects. You may have sensitive skin on your scalp if you have lost your hair during chemo or radiation treatments. You may have redness followed by the formation of tough, crusty scales on your skin or mucous membranes—the lining of, for example, your mouth, esophagus, or rectum—caused by inflammation near the site of your treatment. If your rectum is affected, you may have diarrhea or constipation. These side effects usually occur two to three weeks after you begin treatment and last for approximately four to six weeks. But you can take steps to manage the sensitivities until they go away:

- Leave the area open to the air.

- Make sure dressings don't stick.

- Avoid direct sunlight to the area.

- For diarrhea, avoid spicy foods, eat a low-fiber diet, and drink plenty of fluids.

Throughout treatment and the course of your cancer, your body will undergo many physical changes. Some will be harder to deal with than others. Always let your doctor know if you're in pain or uncomfortable. For physical changes that affect you emotionally, such as weight fluctuations, try to make the best of the situation and know that these things happen as a result of getting better.

ASK YOURSELF THIS

- *Have you seen any physical changes while you have had cancer and undergone treatment? What are they? How do they make you feel?*

- *Have you had pain while dealing with cancer? How did you handle it?*

- *Did you have any side effects from your treatment? What were they, and how did you cope with them?*

- *Has anyone commented about the physical changes you're experiencing? What did they say and how did you react?*

6

I'M SCARED: COPING AND GETTING SUPPORT

"I guess I'm just really overwhelmed," Javier said. "I haven't seen my friends in weeks. No, more like months. I feel too tired to do my schoolwork, and it just doesn't seem to matter in the long run. I know it does,

Cancer support groups are a good place to meet people your age who understand what you're going through.

but I still don't care. And now I have to have more chemo. It's like it'll never end."

It was Javier's first day in his hospital's support group for teens with HL, and he was introducing himself and how he was feeling. His mom had wanted him to go to this support group for weeks, but he wasn't sure if he wanted to talk about gushy feelings with everyone else. He just wanted to get better.

But after last week, when his doctor said he would need yet another round of chemotherapy, he felt completely broken. He would have to stay in the hospital for four more weeks. He just wanted to give up. His doctor and parents saw this change in him and were making him come to the group. *I might as well see how it goes*, Javier thought. *I can't feel any worse*.

After Javier was done talking, a boy across from him named Caleb started talking. "I know how you feel, Javier. I know it's annoying when people say that, because usually they don't, but I really do. I'm on my third round of chemotherapy and am so fed up with everything. If I didn't come to this group to talk about stuff, I'd probably explode."

The group chuckled at this comment. They knew how he felt: that combination of being stressed, scared, frustrated, mad, and just tired of it all. Javier felt a little better after he heard Caleb talk. As they were leaving the group, Javier caught up with him.

"Hey, Caleb, do you want to go to the cafeteria and grab some lunch?"

"Sure," Caleb said.

Javier thought the support group might help after all.

COPING WITH CANCER

Like Javier, you've probably already discovered that cancer doesn't affect just your body; it affects your mind and spirit too. Having cancer is a lot to deal with mentally and emotionally. During the time you have cancer—from diagnosis through being cured—you will feel a wide range of emotions: anger, sadness, loss, denial, hopelessness, and more. It is okay to feel these strong emotions—to be smiling one moment and crying the next. Remember many people will help you through this, including your friends, family, and medical team.

CHANGES AND EMOTIONS

In addition to dealing with physical issues, you'll also be dealing with the emotional impact those changes have. If you have chemo, you will likely lose some or all of your hair, although how much hair you lose depends on what type of

Whether you are more comfortable talking with family, friends, or a counselor, it is really important to talk about what you are going through with somebody.

treatment you get and how your body reacts to it. Some chemo drugs are more likely to cause hair loss or thinning than others. You may even lose hair all over your body. Most often, your hair will grow back, but it may take a while. But that's not very comforting news when you're too embarrassed to go out in public.

There are things you can do to ease any self-conscious feelings you may have. You can shave your head (which is probably cooler if you're a guy), cover it up with a scarf or a hat, or wear a wig. Most treatment centers have information on getting wigs, so ask if you're interested.

Your appearance may have changed in other ways from your surgery, chemo, or radiation. There's nothing you can do to change other people's opinions or reactions to you, so the only thing you can do is change how you feel about your new appearance. Acceptance is the only game in town. Fight, scream, or cry if you have to, but if you want to live in a place of healing and not of bitterness and anger, focus on accepting and loving yourself as you are.

GETTING SUPPORT

It's really important to talk about what you're going through with people closest to you—your family and friends—or even with a counselor. Withdrawing and isolating yourself from others is not a healthy way to deal with your challenges, although you may need to do so once in a while. The good news is that there are many support groups you can go to—both online and in person—when you need help or just want to chat with someone in the same situation.

Ask your doctor or hospital staff about support groups and counseling that are available. Talk with your doctor and parents about setting up an appointment or attending a group. Some kids may not want to talk about their cancer and feelings in person, and that is perfectly okay. There are numerous Web sites, such as Teens Living with Cancer and Group

Loop, that host online forums and discussion groups specifically for teens. You can find others who are in similar situations, ask them your questions, and talk about your concerns. Many teens find, in addition to receiving support, they often support others in these groups and in turn feel better about themselves.

CALMING THE MIND

Feeling fear and anxiety is not abnormal for anyone, both young people and adults, with cancer. The mind is a powerful resource you can utilize to help you through your cancer. Meditation has been shown to help people cope with fear, anxiety, depression, and stress. This and other relaxation techniques such as deep

WARNING SIGNS YOU'RE TOO ISOLATED

If you find that you're experiencing these feelings often, it may be a sign that you need to see someone who can help, such as a counselor or a clergyperson.

- Chronic boredom
- Chronic loneliness
- Depression
- Feeling worthless or empty
- Focusing on negative thoughts
- Keeping your feelings to yourself

Taking steps to reconnect with others and live in the present instead of the past or the future is an important part of your healing process.

Whether you relax by doing yoga, meditating, reading a book, or listening to music, try to do activities that help calm your anxiety.

breathing and guided imagery can calm your mind.

FACING THOUGHTS ABOUT DEATH

From hearing your cancer diagnosis to your journey through treatment, you've probably thought about the possibility of dying. This is natural. Having cancer is like being on an emotional roller coaster. Life is unpredictable. Although most kids your age are thrilled when they get a text message from a crush, you get thrilled when your white blood cell count is normal. But when you find out that chemo isn't working out like your doctor planned and you need to try another round of chemo with different drugs, you come crashing down again and you might think that nothing is going to work.

It's important to note that most kids and teens survive cancer. But, some cancers, especially those in later stages, are incurable. Your feelings of exhaustion, pain, and worry about death might lead to depression and spiritual crisis. If you find yourself feeling this way, always seek help, as many resources are available for you. You can talk with your parents, a minister, a counselor, or another adult you trust. It is important that you talk with someone

THOUGHTS ABOUT DEATH

Thoughts about death and dying can vary greatly. Some kids may think about it a lot, while others don't really think about it at all. Jenny, a girl with ALL, put it this way:

I'm not afraid of dying. . . . I don't fear it. Just because I have cancer doesn't mean I have to die. Each case is different, and each person isn't doomed. Everyone is an individual. If you make it or not, it's what's supposed to happen. Everyone is going to die, you can't change that. The doctors tell me I've got a 30 percent chance of not making it. So what? That doesn't mean anything to me. I don't dwell on it.[1]

Whatever you feel, it is okay. Just remember that you can always talk to someone. Support is always available.

so depression does not consume you. Here are some other suggestions:

- Contact others who have cancer, either in your local support group or on an online discussion board. Share your experiences and find other kids your age who have cancer and are going through some of the same kinds of things as you.

- Keep a journal. Writing down your thoughts can help clarify how you feel and release your emotions instead of keeping them bottled up.

- Talk to your doctor. She or he can answer your medical questions and help you look at likely scenarios from a scientific standpoint. Sometimes focusing on the worst-case scenario is in itself the worst thing.

- Your hospital treatment center can refer you to counselors, clergy, or social workers who are experienced in dealing with issues of death and dying. You should not feel weird about exploring these issues if you want to.

You probably don't look at life the same way you did before you had cancer and now have different priorities. It's important to share those feelings with others who can understand and empathize with what you're going through. You can also share your thoughts about how you're making sense of your experience. It's a way of helping yourself and others.

ASK YOURSELF THIS

- *What emotions are the hardest for you to cope with? Why do you think this is?*

- *How often do you find yourself sad, afraid, or anxious? What do you do when you feel this way?*

- *Have you thought about death and dying before? What do you think about it?*

- *Do you have a support system? Who is in it? How do they help you?*

- *Have you tried meditation or relaxation techniques to calm you and ease your stress? How did it go?*

WARNING SIGNS OF DEPRESSION

Researchers estimate that approximately 15 to 25 percent of all patients with cancer will experience depression.[2] Depression is a serious illness that may require separate treatment. It can also interfere with your recovery. Get help immediately if you experience any of the following symptoms for longer than two weeks:

- Irritability or aggressive behavior
- Crying a lot every day
- Lack of interest in most activities that you once enjoyed
- Trouble sleeping or sleeping too much
- Extreme fatigue, even though your health has improved
- Feeling worthless or helpless
- Thoughts of suicide

I NEED YOU AND MY SPACE: YOUR RELATIONSHIPS

"**D**ad, come on. I'll be okay. I'm just going to go play catch for a while with Malik and Ben," Joey said. "The doctors said it was okay for me to get a little exercise."

7

Having cancer can make family conversations tense sometimes, even during normal activities such as eating dinner.

"Joey, I'm sorry, you just can't go yet. That's final," Joey's dad said.

"Fine. I'll sit in my room and rot. I hope you're happy," Joey said, as he stormed out of the living room.

Ever since Joey was out of the hospital, his dad was not letting him do anything. He couldn't go to the movies last weekend. He couldn't even go play video games at his buddy's house. It was driving him nuts. He'd been out of the hospital for four weeks now. His treatment went well and he was feeling good. His doctors said he could even play baseball—well, at least throw the ball around a little bit. Joey would make sure to stop when he was tired. He wasn't stupid. *Ugh!* His dad was just always by him, hovering. He was always looking out for the smallest side effect or symptom. Why couldn't his dad just get his own life so Joey could have his back.

At dinner, Joey didn't look at or talk to his dad. Finally, his dad spoke. "Joey, I know you're mad, but I'm just trying to look out for you. Your mother and I are just concerned."

"Well that's fine, Dad. I'm concerned too. I am the one with cancer after all. But I need to be able to see my friends. I haven't been able to do anything for months because of this stupid

disease, and now that I can, you're not letting
me. Excuse me," Joey said, as he got up from
the dinner table.

"Joey," his mom stepped in. "You know your
dad loves you and is just trying to protect you.
We will work on letting you be a teenager, but
we'll still be watching out for you."

CHANGING RELATIONSHIPS

Since you've been diagnosed with cancer,
your relationships with other people have most
likely changed. Friends and family may become
closer or more distant. Sometimes your family
or friends expect you to do things that you're
not able to do. Even though you might want to
be super independent, sometimes you're going
to need more help and support or just someone
to listen. Maintaining good communication with

FINDING A NEW NORMAL

Once you have cancer, you may feel like things will never
be "normal" again. This can be really frustrating. Instead
of thinking hopeless thoughts, try putting a different spin
on the situation. Realize that your life *can* be normal again,
but that it'll be a new kind of normal. Sure, you may look
different, but try to embrace it. Think of how you look now
as normal for this part of your life. Your relationships are
changing, but this happens with everyone. Think of it as
a normal part of your own unique existence. A shift in
attitude helps you change your perspective to enjoy the
life you have.

Your parents might not always agree on what is best for you, but they have your best interest in mind. Try to remember this is hard for them too.

your family and friends during your cancer will be good for everyone.

PARENTS

Like Joey, you may feel like your parents are babying you more than ever. Before you had cancer, you were trying to do your own thing. Now, it's even harder, with your parents always watching your every breath and move. You might just need your space. That's okay. If your parents aren't letting you do things even your doctors are okay with, you need to have an open and honest conversation. Let your parents know you love them and appreciate their concern and help, but you need to try being a normal teenager again, which means hanging out with your friends and doing other things.

Maybe you're having the opposite problem Joey has. Maybe one of your parents is being more distant. This could be for a variety of reasons, including that your mom or dad doesn't know how to act or is too scared to be involved in the situation. While it shouldn't be your responsibility to involve them in your life, you can let your parents know when you need them, like during treatment or when you're just really overwhelmed.

SIBLINGS

Just like with your parents, your relationships with your siblings will likely change when you have cancer—for better or for worse. Siblings who were close before the cancer diagnosis may be driven apart by feelings of parental neglect and jealousy. Siblings who had a rough relationship before the cancer now might be very close. There is no single way in which siblings'

> "I didn't want to be a burden on my mom. I didn't want her to think she had to take care of me. I was going to conquer it myself. If I couldn't do it myself, I wasn't going to do it at all."[1]
>
> —Bernadette, teenage cancer patient

Siblings of cancer patients cope with cancer in different ways. Some may draw closer to you and others might pull away. They are scared too.

relationships are affected. As in all relationships, having cancer will probably add stress at certain times. Be aware that your brother or sister probably doesn't hate you if they say they wish you'd go to the hospital. Siblings will all cope differently. Try to remember that when reacting to their actions and words.

FRIENDS

During a time in your life when you might be relying more on friendships than family, cancer can change your relationships with your friends.

A large aspect of teenage life involves finding out where you fit in among your peers and finding good friends. Cancer can make this more challenging. Your appearance will probably change and you might be nervous your friends will reject you. You just want your friends to realize you're still the same person. Only your looks have changed.

Still, some friends may not call you to check up on you, and you may eventually lose them as your friends. Losing friends can really sting, but the good news is that you'll find out who your true friends are during this time. Plus, you'll probably make new friends in the hospital or at a support group you attend.

STAY IN TOUCH DURING TREATMENT

One way to stay in contact with friends during your treatment is to start your own Web site or blog. Write poetry or journal entries and include information about how you're doing and what you're going through. Invite your friends to visit your site. Writing might be an easier way to share this information with your friends too. You can also easily video chat, text, and call your friends to stay in touch.

Many good friends will stick by you through the ups and downs of your cancer.

ASK YOURSELF THIS

- *Have your relationships with your parents changed? How? How do you deal with these changes?*

- *Do you have any siblings? If so, how is having cancer affecting your relationships?*

- *How has cancer affected your friendships?*

- *Have friends or family members ever lashed out at you for getting attention? How did you deal with that?*

8

CLASSMATES AND HOMEWORK: DEALING WITH SCHOOL

Brittany walked through the hall on her first day back to class, trying to keep her hands from constantly adjusting her wig. She had decided to wear a wig instead of a scarf or a hat, praying she would fit in and

Some of your peers might not know how to act around you. Try not to let them affect how you feel about yourself.

no one would really notice her hair looked a bit different.

"Hey, Brit," her friend Sam called. "Excited for algebra? I, for one, cannot wait," Sam said as they walked into class.

The bell chimed. "All right, class, let's begin the period," Mr. Bernard said. "I'd like to welcome back Brittany to school. Although she has been gone for a few months, she's been keeping up on her algebra studies and quite possibly could be much further along than all of us," he joked.

Brittany smiled. Leave it to Mr. Bernard to make her feel at ease, but she could still feel her classmates' eyes on her. She looked around and saw a mixture of questioning and happy faces looking toward her. But she thought she also saw a couple girls whispering and giggling. *Oh, no*, she thought, *they're making fun of how I look*. In addition to her new wig, Brittany had lost a lot of weight and looked almost gaunt.

Throughout the day, Brittany saw people whisper to each other as she walked by. Why wouldn't they just come out and say something instead of making her feel like a leper? After school, Brittany met up with Sam to walk home.

"How'd it go today?" he asked.

"People just had to get used to seeing me look different. I was the same old Jenn. I just had a new look."[1]

—Jenn, 16, on looking different and going back to school after AML

"It was all right, I guess. People kept looking at me and whispering. I could feel people talking about me behind my back, saying I look so weird," Brittany said.

"Don't worry, Brit," Sam said. "You don't look weird. You look a little bit different is all. Just tell me if anyone is mean to you, and I'll take care of them," Sam joked.

Brittany laughed. School wasn't the best today, but she was happy to be back and to have Sam on her side. She knew it would be different for a while, but she thought things would be okay.

SCHOOL IS TOUGH ENOUGH ALREADY

School is stressful. Homework increases with every grade, just as you might be getting into more extracurricular activities. Finding a balance can be challenging. Add in dealing with cancer and school might seem unbearable.

For some teens with cancer, however, school is a welcome distraction. Focusing on learning new things, finding your skills and abilities, and finishing homework may keep your

During treatment you might not have the energy to do homework. Try to focus on your assignment for 30 minutes and then take a break.

mind from overanalyzing everything about your cancer.

ABSENCE FROM SCHOOL

When you first start treatment, you will likely be absent from school for some time. How long you're out of school varies depending on what type of cancer you have and the treatments you need. You could be gone from a couple weeks to a couple years.

While you're gone, it's important to stay in close contact with your teachers and guidance counselors so they know how much work you can handle and so you can stay on track with your assignments. If you miss a lot of school, you may be given an individualized education plan (IEP), which allows for adjusted class schedules and assignments, waives penalties incurred from absences, and sets up tutoring. If you are in the hospital for a while, ask your doctor or nurse what resources are available to you at the hospital. Some hospitals have tutors, while other children's oncology units have educational facilities in the hospital.

IEPs

Getting an education while living with cancer is a legal right all students have. If you cannot attend school, an IEP is the way you will do this. An IEP is set up and agreed upon by the school and your parents or guardians. Your IEP will list your educational goals and objectives while on the plan and provide for extra services, such as counseling, tutoring, independent studies, and possible adjustment of graduation requirements. Your IEP is reviewed each year to make sure the plan is a good fit and is working.

HOMEWORK

Undergoing treatment can take a lot out of your body, and sometimes you might not have the energy to do your homework. Listen to your body and do what you can. For a while, your doctor may say you shouldn't even focus on homework. You may need to focus only on healing. Once you're given the okay to do schoolwork, make the commitment to try doing an assignment for a half hour. If at the end of a half hour you're still too tired, then take a break. If you were hesitant to start your homework because you just didn't want to do it, a half hour gives you enough time to get in the swing of things and focus.

RETURNING TO SCHOOL

As soon as you are able to go back to school, you should. Returning to school will help your life return to your new normal. Even if you can't attend full-time, you can return part-time and work up to full, or remain part-time while undergoing treatment.

One of teens' biggest concerns about returning to school is looking different. If you have lost your hair or your weight has changed a lot, you may be anxious about what your peers will say. Wearing a wig, a hat, or a scarf can help you stand out less. Wearing clothes that fit your body, whether you need to go up or

You may be self-conscious of your new appearance, but the people who matter will realize it's the same you.

down a size, can make you more confident in your appearance. You may still feel weird even after doing these things. Some kids might not talk to you at all or they might whisper about you behind your back, as Brittany noticed. Unfortunately, there's not much you can do about this. Keep your head held high and when you're feeling low, talk with your true friends or a trusted adult.

ASK YOURSELF THIS

- *Has having cancer impacted your education? How?*

- *Were you or are you nervous to return to school? What is your biggest concern?*

- *Do you have adjusted schoolwork or an IEP? How are these adjustments working for you?*

- *What is doing homework like for you now that you have cancer?*

SHARE WHAT YOU WANT

When you return to school, your friends and classmates may have a lot of questions for you. What kind of cancer do you have? What exactly does that mean? How are you feeling? Why do you look different? Can I get you anything? When will you be cured? The questions may seem to go on and on and you may just want to say, "Leave me alone!"

Well, you can do that. You can tell your classmates that you'd rather not talk about your cancer right now, but thank them for asking. Or, you can tell them what's going on. You can let them know more about your type of cancer and the treatments you're going through and how you're feeling. Everyone is different. You get to decide how much you want to share.

9

A BRIGHT FUTURE: AFTER YOUR TREATMENT ENDS

Marquis was terrified when he was first diagnosed with cancer and even more terrified at the prospect of having a bone marrow transplant. He needed high-dose chemo and radiation, but those treatments also destroyed his immune system. So he was pretty

Cancer survivors go on to lead happy, healthy, productive lives.

washed out physically and emotionally, even before his doctor performed the transplant.

After his procedure, Marquis had a high risk of infection, so his doctors had to keep his environment as germ-free as possible. Although he left the hospital, his worries intensified— worries about getting an infection, needing more blood transfusions, going back to school, and more.

Even after the doctors told him he was in remission, he couldn't shake the constant fear that he would relapse. Marquis went back for regular checkups, but before each appointment, he got so nervous he threw up. Finally, when Marquis had been free of cancer for five years, his doctors said he was cured. He was relieved, but he wondered: *Could it come back?*

LIVING CANCER-FREE

Once your treatment is complete and your body is cancer-free, you will continue follow-up appointments at a survivor clinic. Here you'll receive yearly checkups, most likely for the rest of your life. Doctors at the survivor clinic check for side effects of treatment and relapse of cancer. Once you have been cancer-free for five years, doctors consider you cured. Although you

are cured, you can still experience side effects
of treatment.

LATE EFFECTS OF TREATMENT

Doctors can predict fairly accurately what a
treatment's side effects will be and will let you
know what to expect. Most of these side effects
usually go away fairly quickly after treatment is
over. But doctors can't always predict how your
treatments will affect you physically months or
years later.

Symptoms or other issues that occur well
after your treatment is over are called late

FOLLOW-UP VISITS

During your follow-up visits, the National Cancer Institute
recommends that you discuss the following points with
your doctor, when applicable:

- Symptoms that may indicate your cancer has returned
- New or different pain
- Physical problems that affect your quality of life, such as
  fatigue, problems with your bladder or bowels, problems
  with concentration, memory, sleep, or weight gain or loss
- Any medicines, vitamins, or herbs you're taking and any
  other treatments you're using
- Any emotional issues you're having, such as anxiety
  or depression
- Any changes in your family medical history, including
  any new cancers[1]

In between checkups, you may experience symptoms
that make you think your cancer has returned. Be sure to
discuss your symptoms with your doctor, even if you've
just had a checkup. It's important to contact your doctor
right away; don't wait until your next checkup.

effects of treatment. They usually result from chemo or radiation therapy—because these treatments damage healthy cells as well as cancer cells—and may be mild or severe in intensity. Some cancers and their treatments have a higher risk of late effects than others. Late effects can be physical or emotional. If you experience any of the following, tell your current doctors about your cancer and all the treatments you had so they can see if there is a connection.

PHYSICAL AND EMOTIONAL EFFECTS

Although any cancer treatment can lead to health problems later, your risk of developing these effects depends on factors such as the age at which you received your treatment, the location and type of cancer you had, the dosage of radiation or chemo you received, your inherited risk factors for developing certain diseases, and any other health problems you may have. Some of the late effects you might experience can include infertility, nerve damage, heart problems, lung problems, headaches or seizures, memory or attention problems, growth or development problems, hearing or vision problems, learning problems, and behavioral problems.

Late effects can also be emotional and may include depression and anxiety. If your depression is severe or lasts longer than two weeks, it's important to talk to a counselor or other professional. Don't wait and hope things get better.

POSSIBILITY FOR RELAPSE

Like Marquis, many teens who had cancer might be nervous about relapsing, even after becoming a cancer survivor. Relapse occurs when cancer returns after a patient has been in remission or is cured. Relapse can be emotionally draining, often more so than when a patient first had cancer, since the recurrence comes after the patient believed the cancer was successfully beaten. Unfortunately, doctors are unable to tell if you will relapse. If you have any concerns or questions about it, talk to your doctor.

FINDING HOPE AND MEANING IN YOUR EXPERIENCE

Now that you've survived your cancer, you probably feel like a very different person than you were before being diagnosed. Your priorities and needs have changed—maybe even your values. You have confronted your strengths and your weaknesses. Fighting cancer may have helped you clarify what you really believe in and who you really are. These experiences and changes have

After you've gone into remission or have been cured, regular checkups will remain an important part of your life.

made you who you are today and affect who you become in the future.

Although they usually didn't feel this way at the time, many people who have lived through cancer have said their disease was the best thing that ever happened to them. Why would they say such a bizarre thing? Because without cancer, they wouldn't have learned all the valuable lessons their cancer had to teach them—the beauty of living in the present moment, the love of friends and family, the joy in simple pleasures such as eating their favorite foods or enjoying a day in the sunshine—things that they, and you, may have taken for granted before cancer. Cancer survivors often feel as if they've gained far more than they've lost.

FINDING MEANING AND MOVING FORWARD

A boy named Alex was diagnosed with ALL at the end of seventh grade. Once he had recovered, his mom asked him, "If you could go back and trade it all in for a chance at a normal life, would you?" He said, "Never in a million years would I trade this experience in. Knowing what kind of person I am today, knowing the tremendous amounts of people going through this ordeal, knowing the other side of life, knowing people who are not ordinary people—heroes in my eyes—and knowing the power I hold in my hands to make a difference in the world. I'd do it again in a heartbeat."[2]

ASK YOURSELF THIS

- *Has your doctor talked to you about late effects of your treatment? What did he or she tell you might be possible for you to experience? How do you feel about that?*

- *Have you experienced any late effects? What are they? How are you dealing with them?*

- *Have you talked with your doctor about your cancer recurring? What did he or she tell you? How do you feel?*

- *What do you think and how do you feel about your future?*

- *How has having cancer changed you for the better?*

JUST THE FACTS

Cancer is difficult to define because it's not just one disease. Many different types of cancer exist.

All types of cancers are similar in some ways. The process always starts with a single cell. But, many things have to go wrong in your body to create each kind of cancer. So each cancer is unique.

The cancers teens develop are different from those adults often develop. What causes teen cancer is not fully known.

More than 80 percent of teens who develop cancer survive.

Some of the main symptoms of the kinds of cancers teens get include lumps or bumps on the body that don't go away, unusual pain or swelling in any part of the body, severe fatigue, shortness of breath, loss of appetite, excessive bleeding or bruising, frequent infections, severe or frequent headaches, changes in speech, changes in vision, changes in hearing, and problems with balance.

Leukemias are cancers of the blood, while lymphomas are cancers of the lymphatic system. In young people ages ten to 14, leukemias are the most common form of cancer; older teens tend to get lymphomas most often.

Your family doctor or pediatrician is the one who is most likely to discover your cancer first because you see that doctor most often.

The most common tests you'll need to diagnose your cancer are blood tests, imaging studies such as X-rays or CT scans, and a biopsy.

Although there are many specialized treatments for cancer, the most common treatments are chemotherapy, radiation therapy, and surgery.

Learning how to manage your cancer treatment involves dealing with yourself as a whole person—your mind, body, and spirit.

Dealing with cancer can be overwhelming. Many in-person and online support groups, as well as counselors, are available to help you through these times.

Relationships with family and friends will likely change. Good communication is important in maintaining these relationships through challenging times.

An IEP can help you with schoolwork if you are missing a lot of school.

Doctors can't always predict how your treatments will affect you physically months or years later. Problems that may crop up later are called the late effects of treatment and may result from the cancer itself or from chemo or radiation treatments.

WHERE TO TURN

If You Want More Information about Treatments

If you've been diagnosed with cancer, and your doctor told you that you need chemotherapy to shrink your tumor before your surgery, you may be worried about what's in store for you. You've heard about the side effects of chemo, but you're not sure about what kinds of drugs are used for your kind of cancer or if you'll get really sick and lose all your hair. You may have an appointment with your oncologist to talk more about your treatment, but in the meantime, you'd like to get more information from a trusted source. You can contact several Web sites and organizations to get more information, including the American Cancer Society, www.cancer.org, and the Children's Oncology Group, www.curesearch.org.

If You Want to Talk with Other Kids in the Same Situation

If you're being treated for cancer, and you're in the hospital or you feel really isolated at home, it might help you a lot to communicate with other kids who are going through the same thing you are. You may want to know how they're dealing with treatment and what their thoughts and feelings are about having cancer. Or you may just want to talk with some kids your own age who understand your situation. Your body has changed, and you're not quite the same person you used to be. You feel differently about life, but you're afraid your friends won't understand what you've been through. Know that there are kids out there who are feeling the same way as you. They'd be happy to connect with you and share their stories and hear yours. A few of the places you can go to connect with other kids with cancer are Youth Health Talk, www.youthhealthtalk.org, Teens Living with Cancer, www.teenslivingwithcancer.org, Kids Cancer Network, kidscancernetwork.org, and Group Loop, www.grouploop.org.

If You Want to Be in a Clinical Trial

You've learned about clinical trials for cancer, and you're interested in being in one. Although your oncologist is the first person you should talk to about trials, you may find some information on the kinds of trials going on for your particular type of cancer on your own. You may have questions about how to find the trials, how you qualify for them, if they can be dangerous, and if there are any trials going on in your area. There are many different trials involving conventional as well as integrative/complementary medicine. Check out the following organizations and sites: National Cancer Institute's Clinical Trials Home Page, www.cancer.gov/clinicaltrials, National Coalition of Cancer Cooperative Groups, www.cancertrialshelp.org, and Children's Oncology Group, www.curesearch.org.

To Find out More about Keeping Your Body Nourished

If you're being treated for cancer, you know proper nutrition is key to preventing fatigue and keeping up your weight and your strength. You may be able to eat a little, or you may be nauseated a lot and have lost your appetite completely. You may be wondering about where you can go to get more information on the kinds of foods that might be easy on your stomach. You may want to find some recipes. There are many Web sites you can turn to when you need to know about getting the right nutrition before, during, and after cancer treatment. A few Web sites you can visit are the American Institute for Cancer Research, www.aicr.org/site/PageServer, the National Cancer Institute, www.cancer.gov/cancertopics/pdq/supportivecare/nutrition/Patient, and Cancer Nutrition Center, www.cancernutrition.com.

GLOSSARY

anesthesia
The loss of sensation in the body, with or without loss of consciousness.

astrocytes
Types of brain cells.

benign
Not cancerous.

bone graft
A piece of bone from a patient's body that takes the place of removed bone.

chemotherapy
The treatment of cancers or infections with drugs that have a toxic effect on the cause of the illness.

clinical trials
Medical research studies that involve humans and test the effectiveness of drugs or medical treatments.

deoxyribonucleic acid (DNA)
The molecular basis of heredity; the genetic material that determines a cell's growth and reproduction.

five-year relative survival rate
The percentage of people who survive at least five years after a cancer diagnosis.

intravenous
The administration of a drug directly into a vein.

malignant
Cancerous.

metastasis
The spread of cancer to another organ.

neurologist
A doctor who specializes in diagnosing and treating diseases of the nervous system, which includes the brain, spinal cord, nerves, and muscles.

oncologist
A doctor who treats cancer.

prognosis
The outlook of recovery for a disease.

radiation therapy
The treatment of cancer using radiation.

relapse
A recurrence of symptoms of a disease after a period of improvement.

remission
A decrease in the signs and symptoms of a disease; a remission may be partial or complete.

steroids
Hormones that perform a variety of functions in the body, from regulating the immune system to decreasing inflammation.

ventricles
Cavities in the brain that are filled with fluid.

ADDITIONAL RESOURCES

SELECTED BIBLIOGRAPHY

Bruning, Nancy. *Coping with Chemotherapy.* New York: Penguin, 2002. Print.

Harpham, Wendy Schlessel. *Diagnosis Cancer: Your Guide Through the First Few Months.* New York: Norton, 1998. Print.

Hersh, Stephen P. *Beyond Miracles: Living with Cancer.* Lincolnwood, IL: Contemporary, 1998. Print.

Silver, Julie K. *After Cancer Treatment: Heal Faster, Better, Stronger.* Baltimore, MD: Johns Hopkins UP, 2006. Print.

FURTHER READINGS

Baker, Lynn S. *You and Leukemia: A Day at a Time.* Philadelphia, PA: W. B. Saunders, 2001. Print.

Bakewell, Lisa, and Karen Bellenir, eds. *Cancer Information for Teens: Health Tips About Cancer Awareness, Prevention, Diagnosis, and Treatment.* Detroit, MI: Omnigraphics, 2010. Print.

Thornton, Denise. *Living with Cancer: The Ultimate Teen Guide.* Lanham, MD: Scarecrow, 2011. Print.

WEB LINKS

To learn more about living with cancer visit ABDO Publishing Company online at **www.abdopublishing.com**. Web sites about living with cancer are featured on our Book Links page. These links are routinely monitored and updated to provide the most current information available.

SOURCE NOTES

CHAPTER 1. I HAVE WHAT? CANCER BASICS

1. "Most Cancer Is NOT Inherited." *National Cancer Institute*. National Cancer Institute, 1 Sep. 2006. Web. 2 Feb. 2011.

2. "Childhood Cancer Statistics." *American Childhood Cancer Organization*. American Childhood Cancer Organization, n.d. Web. 2 Feb. 2011.

3. Ibid.

CHAPTER 2. FINDING OUT FOR SURE: TESTS AND DIAGNOSIS

1. Gail B. Stewart. *Teens with Cancer*. San Diego, CA: Lucent, 2002. Print. 33.

2. Ibid. 9.

CHAPTER 3. DID I DO SOMETHING WRONG? CANCER IN TEENS

1. "Childhood Blood Cancers." Leukemia & Lymphoma Society of Canada. *Leukemia & Lymphoma Society of Canada*, 3 Apr. 2011. Web. 15 July 2011.

2. "Childhood Blood Cancers." Leukemia & Lymphoma Society. *Leukemia & Lymphoma Society*, 23 Mar. 2011. Web. 15 July 2011.

3. Ibid.

4. Ibid.

5. Ibid.

6. "Hodgkin Lymphoma." Leukemia & Lymphoma Society. *Leukemia & Lymphoma Society*, 23 Mar. 2011. Web. 15 July 2011.

7. Peter J. Buecker, Mark Gebhardt, and Kristy Weber. "Osteosarcoma." *Liddy Shriver Sarcoma Institute*. Liddy Shriver Sarcoma Institute, 2005. Web. 2 Feb. 2011.

8. "Bone Cancer FAQ: List of Questions (Osteosarcoma)." *Cancer Index*. Cancer Index, 17 May 2003. Web. 2 Feb. 2011.

9. "Bone Cancer FAQ: List of Questions (Ewing's Sarcoma/PNET)." *Cancer Index*. Cancer Index, 17 May 2003. Web. 2 Feb. 2011.

10. "Ewing's sarcoma." *MedlinePlus*. U.S. National Library of Medicine, 2 Mar. 2010. Web. 2 Feb. 2011.

11. "Rhabdomyosarcoma." *Liddy Shriver Sarcoma Institute*. Liddy Shriver Sarcoma Institute, 2004. Web. 2 Feb. 2011.

12. "Childhood Rhabdomyosarcoma." *MD Anderson Cancer Center.* University of Texas MD Anderson Cancer Center, n.d. Web. 2 Feb. 2011.

CHAPTER 4. GETTING RID OF YOUR CANCER: TREATMENT

1. "Nutrition in Cancer Care." *National Cancer Institute*. National Cancer Institute, 12 Sept. 2009. Web. 2 Feb. 2011.

2. "Fighting Malnutrition Among Cancer Patients." *Medical News TODAY*. MediLexicon International, 19 July 2007. Web. 2 Feb. 2011.

SOURCE NOTES CONTINUED

CHAPTER 5. I DON'T FEEL SO WELL: THE EFFECTS OF TREATMENT

None.

CHAPTER 6. I'M SCARED: COPING AND GETTING SUPPORT

1. Elena Dorfman. *The C-Word: Teenagers and Their Families Living with Cancer*. Portland, OR: NewSage, 1994. Print. 30.

2. "Depression After Cancer." *Yale Cancer Center*. Yale Cancer Center, n.d. PDF file. 2 Feb. 2011.

CHAPTER 7. I NEED YOU AND MY SPACE: YOUR RELATIONSHIPS

1. Karen Gravelle and Bertram A. John. *Teenagers Living with Cancer*. New York: Simon & Schuster, 1986. Print. 51.

CHAPTER 8. CLASSMATES AND HOMEWORK: DEALING WITH SCHOOL

1. "Going Back to School." *Teens Living with Cancer*. Teens Living with Cancer, n.d. Web. 13 June 2011.

CHAPTER 9. A BRIGHT FUTURE: AFTER TREATMENT ENDS

1. "Follow-up Care After Cancer Treatment." *National Cancer Institute*. National Cancer Institute, 17 May 2010. Web. 2 Feb. 2011.

2. Adam. "I Wouldn't Trade It." *CureSearch for Children's Cancer*. CureSearch, n.d. Web. 1 July 2011.

INDEX

ABOUT THE AUTHOR

Genevieve T. Slomski, PhD, a freelance writer and editor living in Connecticut, is the author of a variety of essays, articles, and book chapters on medicine, literature, and the arts.

PHOTO CREDITS